LIFE INSURANCE MASTERY: SELLING LIKE A PRO

THE ULTIMATE GUIDE TO LIFE INSURANCE SALES

HARBANS LAL ARORA

Contents

Foreword   *v*

Preface   *ix*

Acknowledgements   *xi*

Secret Mantras For Selling Like A Pro

1. Find Your Why   3
2. What Is MDRT   5
3. Convert Your Goal Into SMART Goal   6
4. Raise The Bar   7
5. Follow OAR Model   8
6. Visualise The Achievement Of Goal   10
7. Declare Your SMART Goal   12
8. Divide Your Goal Input & Output Wise   13
9. Find Out A Mentor   15
10. Review Your Performance   16
11. Find Out Your Success Formula   17
12. Be Consistent   19
13. Learn, Unlearn & Relearn   20
14. Identify The Right Target Segment   21
15. Networking   24
16. Find Out Your Niche   26
17. Know Your Customer   27
18. Diversification   29
19. Use The Power Of Recommendations   30
20. Sell Yourself Well   31
21. Use Social Media   32
22. Elevator Pitch   33

Contents

23. The Art Of Probing   35

24. Listening Matters   37

25. Emotional Disturbance   38

26. Win The Trust   39

27. Adapt Technology   40

28. Train More To Learn More   41

29. Time Management   42

30. Use The Power Of Delegation   43

31. Seva Bhav (Selfless Service)   44

32. Celebrate Every Milestone   45

33. Never Say Die Spirit   46

Modern Era Life Insurance Sales Process - Selling Like A Pro

34. Prospecting   49

35. Approaching   52

36. Meet The Prospect & Need Analysis   56

37. Preparing & Presenting The Solution   67

38. Closing   70

39. Reference Taking   75

40. Customer Service   77

41. Objection Handling   79

Abbreviations   85

Disclaimer   87

How To Contact The Author   89

Foreword

Ashwani Kumar Shukla
Insurance Veteran,
FIII (Fellowship from Insurance Institute of India)

Hi,

Selling life insurance is more than just closing a deal — it's about protecting dreams and securing futures. However, mastering the art of life insurance sales requires more than just product knowledge; it demands the right mindset, approach, and skills.

"Life Insurance Mastery - Selling Like A Pro" is a practical guide designed to help you excel in the life insurance industry. It covers proven sales techniques, the complete sales process, and strategies to build trust and close deals with confidence. Whether you are new to the profession or a seasoned advisor, this book will equip you to sell with purpose and impact.

Read it, apply it, and watch your career soar.

Thanks and Regards,

Ashwani Kumar Shukla

Anurag Shrivastava
Executive Vice President & Business Head
(Head of Agency & Broking)
Aviva Life Insurance Company India Ltd.

Dear Readers,

I met Harbans in 2008 when he joined my team as Training Head. After that we worked together for many years. A dediicated and highly passionate insurance sales professional cum trainer who has the zeal, enthusiasm and determination to contribute to life insurance sales professionals in their growth and development of professionals in the industry.

His training programs created hundreds of high producing and high earning sales professionals both Distributors and Employees. How to Create and mentor MDRTs is his forte. His previous book on life insurance selling "Sell Life Insurance Proudly" was a superhit.

His mission of "Die Empty" is visible through this 2nd book for life insurance professionals. This book **"Life Insurance Mastery: Selling Like A Pro"** is a complete guide for life insurance sales people and would say is a must for all Sales Professionals.

Using illustrations and examples collected over a very long term spent training people in the field of insurance will give readers the disciplines, the techniques, the concepts and the process of achieving success in the field of insurance selling. This is a practical book to be applied in the field. You will get immediate results from the techniques explained in this wonderful book.

It will empower the sales professionals to achieve top goals of their career like creating and achieving MDRT, COT and TOT. It will ensure that they develop the required skill and mind set to be the top sales professionals of life insurance industry so that they get best of the recognition, high earnings and a respected status of top life insurance sales professional. I am sure that readers will be immensely benefitted with book.

My best wishes to Harbans for his contribution to spread awareness on life insurance with his books.

I recommend this book for each and every life insurance sales professional.

Go all out & buy this book today itself.

Regards,

Anurag

Preface

During my childhood, I saw my elder brother working as LIC agent for a few years. I observed him very closely while he pitched life insurance policies to his prospects. I also came to know about a relative where life insurance claim money helped the family a lot when the main bread earner passed away.

Insurance was one of my subjects during my B.Com. days & I took a lot of interest to understand the nitty gritty of insurance. After that, I completed my MBA in 2000.

I joined the corporate world in 2000. It was the same year when a few of the private insurance companies got the licence from the IRDAI.

I got my calling for life insurance sector in Nov 2001. I started my life insurance journey as a Unit Manager for rural sector in the surrounding area of Faridabad. My role was to recruit & develop a team of 30 plus life insurance advisors from the rural belt of Faridabad.

I feel blessed that I got best of the training inputs during those days. Same was true for my advisors. It helped us to perform better. Within next 1 year, I moved to urban sales. My new office was in Gurugram, Haryana.

Here I saw the real power & scale of life insurance business. I witnessed how normal ordinary people were becoming MDRT advisors, qualifying for various national & international conventions. I also witnessed the earning scope when many of our advisors earned more than the salaries of top management people.

I realised why people called it a noble profession. I moved to a trainer role in 2004 in life insurance industry, my last role was a national head training till Dec 2020.

From Jan 2021 onwards, I started my new journey of a corporate trainer, motivational trainer & an author. In last 21 years, I got an opportunity to empower more than 100000 life insurance advisors. Many of them qualified for MDRT level or various clubs announced internally for various life insurance companies. This was a two-way learning. These people shared their success mantras to achieve MDRT & above.

This book is a culmination of those success mantras shared by thousands of MDRT / club qualifiers. It will be useful to all those people who want to achieve success in life insurance selling, qualify for MDRT & above levels or who want to create MDRTs in their teams.

I have taken a mission of "Die Empty." Keeping this in mind, my first book on life insurance titled as "Sell Life Insurance Proudly" was published in Feb 2024. If you have not bought it then do order it today. It's available through Amazon, Flipkart & Notion Press. It consists of 51 sales ideas, stories & activities to sell life insurance proudly.

This book is another effort to continue the same mission. This book is a step-by-step guide to achieve MDRT or other club qualifications offered by various life insurance companies. While this book is for life insurance professionals however the same can be applicable to health & general insurance professionals with some tweaks.

How to read & use this book – Go from the beginning till end chapter wise. At the end of a few chapters, there is some space given for writing your actionable. Write it immediately after reading these chapters if it's applicable to you. If you have bought kindle version then you can write these actionable separately in your notebook or in digital format.

Reading these lines also shows that you are serious for these milestones & are ready to take the required actions for the same. Please accept my congratulations in advance to become a MDRT advisor & above. Wish you many more successes in this profession. More power to you. Lots of love & best wishes.

Acknowledgements

I would like to specially mention the name of **Jyoti Arora** who is better half in every sense and true inspiration behind writing this book. She stood like a wall in every up and down of life. Both daughters – **Khyati Arora** and **Himanya Arora** were partnering in every aspect of life. They are the true back bone behind the launch of this book.

I would like to say a special thanks to all my supervisors, colleagues, team members, trainers, advisors, leaders, clients and other stakeholders for their contribution in my life.

My sincere thanks to all those people who shared these secret mantras, sales process etc. through social media, public meetings, through books, articles or through training programs.

I acknowledge the contribution of **Ashwani Kumar Shukla & Anurag Shrivastava** for writing **foreword** of this book.

Secret Mantras for selling like a Pro

As per the Pareto principle, 20% of the top sales people contribute 80% of the sales. The same is true for life insurance sales professionals. These top 20% sales people are "Pro" in every sense.

They must be doing something differently from other people. This book is an effort to culminate those secret mantras which worked for them & it can work for you.

In coming chapters, we are going to share those secret mantras for selling like a "Pro." **Are you ready to become a "Pro" in life insurance selling?**

Find Your Why

You need to find out your "WHY" for MDRT / Club Qualification or other goals. Ask yourself, why should I become a MDRT? What's in it for me.

There are various reasons people choose to become a MDRT e.g.:

• **Money**: You earn more money as first year commission & renewal commission. More money can fulfil hundreds of yours & your family dreams. MDRT means that your earning is minimum a million rupees in a calendar year for Indian market. Indirectly, you also qualify for various contests which means more income for you.

• **Rewards**: You can qualify for various domestic & international training conventions. You are eligible to register for MDRT annual meeting which is held every year in June. The MDRT annual meeting gathers thousands of members from around the world to create an exclusive event like no other that stimulates growth through learning, networking, and sharing innovative ideas. 2025 qualifiers will get an opportunity to the MDRT annual meeting at Anaheim, California, USA during Jun 2026. Same way, there are other exclusive events for the qualifying members like MDRT global conference, top of the table annual meeting etc.

• **Personal Branding**: You create a personal brand for yourself. It makes you more professional & trustworthy. You get an opportunity to stand in top 2% of life insurance agents across life insurance industry. This is one of the biggest tags. It's like Oscar of life insurance industry.

• **Networking**: When you attend various domestic & international events, you network with other life insurance professionals & increase your networking. Do remember, your network is your net worth.

• **To empower people**: You are empowering people to live a peaceful life. Life insurance provides that peace of mind to people & removes a lot of insecurities.

• **A cause to live & contribute**: It also provides a "Cause" to live & contribute in the lives of thousands of people.

• **Employment**: For many people, it's an employment or profession like many other professions. It gives them a full or part time employment depending upon the requirement.

• **Respect & Recognition**: You get more respect & recognition from the society. You feel satisfied & happy.

• **Pride**: It's a pride moment for many to achieve the top level in any field. You feel proud to become a MDRT advisor.

There can be many more **"Whys"** behind achieving MDRT milestone. You need to find out your "Why". It can be one or more than one causes like given above.

Initially, it may be tuff to identify the exact why but it will be easier for you once you work for a few months in this industry. A stronger why helps you to achieve this goal with ease. E.g. My Why to write this book is "Die Empty."

What's your Why to become a MDRT / Club Qualification? Write it here (you can change it later on if required)

....

....

....

CHAPTER TWO

What is MDRT

Founded in 1927, Million Dollar Round Table (MDRT) is a global, independent association of the world's leading life insurance & financial services professionals from more than 500 companies in 70 nations & territories.

MDRT members demonstrates exceptional professional knowledge, strict ethical conduct & outstanding client service.

Source: www.mdrt.org

Qualification criteria for MDRTs in India:

• **Production Period**: It's a full calendar year e.g. 1st Jan 2025 to 31st Dec 2025

• **Premium Weightage**: Regular premium - 100% weightage and Single Premium - 6% weightage

• **MDRT premium criteria for 2025**: Rs 45,30,400 Or

• **MDRT commission criteria for 2025**: Rs 11,32,600 (It's 25% of the premium amount)

• **COT (Court of the Table)**: 3 Times of the MDRT numbers

• **TOT (Top of the Table)**: 6 times of the MDRT or 2 times of COT

Refer to www.mdrt.org for the latest criteria, events & other details

• You can qualify either on premium basis or commission basis. You can also decide a goal like single MDRT, double MDRT, Rs 1 crore premium or Rs 25 lakh commission & so on. Ask yourself - I want to qualify on premium or commission basis?

What is my goal for this calendar year? Answer it here

....

CHAPTER THREE

Convert your goal into SMART goal

Check whether your goal is a SMART goal or not.
SMART means:

- S – Specific
- M – Measurable
- A – Achievable
- R – Realistic
- T – Time bound

Only goal setting will not help you but SMART goal setting will help you. Convert your goal into the definition of SMART goal e.g. I want to do MDRT is a goal however it's not a SMART goal. SMART goal will be – I want to achieve MDRT on premium basis by 31st Dec 2025.

What is your SMART goal? Write it here

....

CHAPTER FOUR

Raise the Bar

Ask a question from yourself. The SMART goal decided me is the best goal which I can achieve or can I raise the bar?

E.g. If you qualified for MDRT in the last year, are you still going for MDRT for this year? Can't you go for 1.5 times of MDRT or 2 times of MDRT or COT for this year?

Another example, if you qualified for MDRT in the last year in Dec i.e. in full 12 months, can you raise the bar by achieving this goal in 9 / 10 / 11 months?
    Why to get satisfied while you can raise the bar & create / break your own records.

Take a self-challenge of raising the bar & write your final SMART goal here

....

CHAPTER FIVE

Follow OAR Model

Imagine, you want to sell a life insurance policy & you are not getting desired results. What will you do? Think before you read further.

Have you thought to take more actions e.g. a greater number of telephonic calls, meetings with the prospects? Getting equipped with more skills like objection handling, negotiation skills, probing etc.?

A few people may get better results but many people still struggle for the desired results. I was also in the similar situation a few years back. I was supposed to do coaching calls with my participants & found that most of my participants were either not picking up phone during the fixed coaching call slots or they were not responding the way I expected.

It felt frustrating. I approached my supervisor to find out a solution for the same & in return, found a very unique concept which helped me to overcome the above problem & many more problems. Here is the concept which was shared by my supervisor & it's helping me till date.

The concept is OAR (Observer, Action, Result) model. We all wants results, if we don't get the desired results then we take more actions to get more results e.g., in my case, I tried calling more &

more people for coaching calls however it does not work in this way.

The key is hidden in the first word of this concept i.e. **observer** – means what's going in your mind as observer e.g., when I was calling my participants for coaching calls, I was taking it as extra task forced by my company on me & I always wished that my participants should not pick my phone calls or I did not show much interest even when they picked up my phone. At surface level, I justified myself that I tried to call participants for coaching calls but they are not responding.

Observer changed after my call with my supervisor, I thought that my company is giving me a chance to become a coach & they are assigning coaches on a trust that I will make a difference in their life. I called again these participants during such time slots when they were available; arranged alternate numbers & showed a lot of interest to genuinely empower them. Things started moving in the positive direction. We started getting many success stories & more participants started calling me / responding due to word of mouth. I loved this concept & trained many of my team members on the same. It worked every time.

I invite you to attempt this concept in your personal & professional life. Focus on your observer before you take a first step to achieve this SMART goal. **Trust yourself that you can achieve this SMART goal, don't laugh or doubt at yourself.** People like you did it earlier & will keep doing it in future too.

CHAPTER SIX

Visualise the Achievement of Goal

You already have decided your SMART goal, it's time to visualise the achievement of this goal.

Meet more & more qualifiers who already achieved this goal. Ask them about their experience on it. See their videos / photos or videos released by your company / YouTube channel on the same.

Visualise yourself as one of the qualifiers in the next event. Visualise, what are you wearing in the upcoming event. In which country / city, will you visit once you qualify for the same. Keep those photos as your screen savers or in your bedroom / drawing room / workstation etc. See YouTube videos of the country & city where you are expecting a visit after the qualification.

You are a sum total of 5 people around you so choose your friends carefully. If you are surrounded by MDRT / COT / TOT throughout the year, you are also going to be the next MDRT / COT / TOT. You are giving signals to the universe about your eagerness to achieve it.

If bigger goal is MDRT then by when I will achieve half MDRT & will experience any event organised by the company for such qualifiers. **Show your passion** to achieve such milestones before the deadline.

Keep your passport ready. Apply for it if you don't have passport. Renew it if it's going to expire within next 6 months. Keep yourself fully ready. Don't leave any doubt in your mind that you will not qualify for it.

CHAPTER SEVEN

Declare your SMART goal

Once you have decided the SMART goal, declare it.

Understand the power of declaration:

• You feel more committed
• It puts more pressure on you to achieve the desired SMART goal
• It helps you to attract positive vibes from the universe to achieve your SMART goal
• Other people can feel your seriousness about the SMART goal & can support you to achieve it

You can declare it through social media platforms or one to one. You can also put a declaration board in front of your work station or at a prominent place in your home. It can become your digital profile, screen saver or your password. Share your goal with maximum people like your team leader, branch managers, customers etc.

I am using the power of declaration from last 20 years & found it highly useful. I announced the publishing of this book through one of my LinkedIn posts, 3 months before the actual publishing. Sometimes, I felt to drop the idea of publishing this book but my declaration helped me to write & publish this book.

How will you declare your SMART goal & by when? Write it here

....

Divide your goal input & output wise

While MDRT is a big goal & you will take time to achieve it. Divide this goal into smaller achievable goals e.g. if you want to achieve MDRT on premium basis, you can divide the entire goal in 12 months which becomes approx. Rs 3,77,533 premium per month. You can divide it week wise & day wise too.

Remember, you don't have direct control on the premium but you have a control on the input activities which leads to the premium. You need to find out your input targets on daily, weekly, monthly, quarterly & yearly basis.

If you are targeting your goal on commission basis then you can covert this goal into premium numbers e.g. if you earn average commission of 25% then multiply your commission target with 4 & so on.

Let me share a simple calculator which will help you to track both output & input numbers with an example:

A: Declared SMART Goal Premium Amount: Rs 50,00,000

B: Actual premium done till Now: Rs 10,00,000

C: Required Premium amount to achieve the goal: Rs 40,00,000 (A – B i.e. 50,00,000 – 10,00,000)

D: Expected Average regular Premium / Policy: Rs 1,00,000

E: Number of Closure / policies Required: 40 (C / D i.e. 40,00,000 / 1,00,000)

F: Meeting to Conversion Ratio: 25% (Means if you meet 4 people one to one, you get 1 policy)

G: Total Meetings Required: 160 (E / F i.e. 40 / 25%)

H: Number of months left to achieve the goal: 10

I: Total meetings required / month: 16 (G / H i.e. 160 / 10)

J: Total meetings required / week: 4 (I / 4 i.e. 16 / 4 considering 4 weeks per month)

Do this calculation for yourself through the given format:

A: Declared SMART Goal Premium Amount: Rs ....

B: Actual premium done till Now: Rs ....

C: Required Premium amount to achieve the goal: Rs ....(A – B)

D: Expected Average regular Premium / Policy: Rs ....

E: Number of Closure / policies Required: .... (C / D)

F: Meeting to Conversion Ratio: .....

G: Total Meetings Required: .... (E / F)

H: Number of months left to achieve the goal: ....

I: Total meetings required / month: .... (G / H)

J: Total meetings required / week: .... (I / 4)

You can calculate the same on daily basis, dividing this number by 7 or number of working days as per your preference. You can calculate output goal of number of policies & premium too on weekly & monthly basis.

Good going so far. I appreciate that you are doing these calculations for yourself. It shows how serious you are to achieve these SMART goals.

CHAPTER NINE

Find out a Mentor

You have decided your SMART goal but you may miss the accountability towards this goal.

You can find out a partner / mentor who can push you for this goal, who can help you to review & take corrective action for this goal.

Who can be this partner / mentor:

o Anybody from the family like your spouse, parents, kids, sibling, extended family
o Your office colleagues
o Your supervisors / leaders
o Your friends
o An experience person from the industry like your branch trainer / branch manager / regional / zonal heads etc.

They need to have a genuine interest in your success & not in your competition.
You can fix a review frequency with them & share your success & struggles with them.
You need to be open to take critical feedback & working on the area of improvements.
Who will be my mentor & by when I will finalize the same?
1. ....

CHAPTER TEN

Review your Performance

Many people are good in planning but they don't review the performance required to achieve the goals. If you are seriously looking to achieve your goal, then take out time to review your input & output numbers on weekly, monthly, quarterly basis.

You can also request your team leader, mentor, colleague or a family member to do this review of your performance. You can also do self-review.

Please see the sample review format given. You can create the similar format in the excel sheet or spreadsheet or notepad, as you feel comfortable. You can add any other criteria in it as per the requirement. Your next week goal may change due to the actual achievements of the last week.

Go deeper in the assumed ratios like meeting to conversion ratio & change it if required. Use your analytical skills to find out the gap areas. Take guidance of your mentors for the same.

Criteria	Weekly goal	Achievement	% Achievement	Remarks
Premium	100000	70000	70%	Low Ticket Size
Policies	1	1	100%	Achieved it
Meetings	4	5	125%	Overachieved it

Sample Review Format

CHAPTER ELEVEN

Find out your Success Formula

For every output, you need some inputs. Life insurance business also works in the same way. You can call it success formula or funnel management.

Let me share the success formula for an average life insurance seller:

- 10 prospects lead to
- 5 telephone appointments lead to
- 3 meetings lead to
- 1 closure or policy sell

It can differ depending upon on your experience, target market, your skills etc. You can keep improvising on it.

If you require 10 closures in a month, you require 30 meetings, 50 telephone appointments & 100 prospect names.

It all starts with prospects to whom you can approach to meet. Most of the life insurance seller leave this industry in the first year itself as they don't know how to keep getting the flow of prospects month on month. They use their natural market prospects in the initial 2-3 months & then they get stuck to find out more prospects.

Prospecting is an art & science to keep getting new qualified prospects regularly who can either give you insurance business or refer more customers or become centre of influence etc. In one of the coming chapters, we will share a few ways of prospecting.

Your role is to trust the process & execute it by heart. Process is not on test but you are on test.

Go deeper, calculate your weekly & monthly input goals on number of prospects required, telephone appointment or meetings etc.

Control the controllable, you have control on inputs & not on output. Output will happen automatically if you do the right input. It's like a dice; you can throw a dice, any of the numbers from 1 to 6 can come. Treat number 6 as policy closure, it may come in the first chance, 5th chance or 10th chance but it will come for sure. If you don't throw the dice at all then 6 will never come.

CHAPTER TWELVE

Be Consistent

I have personally observed that most of the MDRT agents are consistent. They do the same things again & again without getting bored or giving up in between.

Success comes to those who are consistent. MDRT is not a journey of only 1 year, it will motivate you to qualify for the same again & again.

Start small e.g. start with just 1 meeting per day or 1 meeting every alternate day but continue this practice. You will do 30 / 15 meetings per month if you continue this practice of one meeting per day or every alternate day. You can increase the frequency once you achieve your first goal consistently for 21 days.

Just to share with you, I continuously posted LinkedIn articles from Sep 2021 till the publishing of this book on every Thursday & Sunday which is equal to around 6 self help books of 30000 words. That's the power of consistency.

Your prospects are testing your consistency. They want to do business only with those sales people who are consistent.

Ask your self - Am I consistent? If not, what's stopping me to become a consistent sales person. Write it here.

....

CHAPTER THIRTEEN

Learn, Unlearn & Relearn

These 3 words are crucial for this industry due to the frequent changes in it. Sometimes there are regulatory changes, sometimes it's technological changes, process changes, changes due to the changing times & so on.

If you are rigid to change & you struggle a lot to adapt then it will be very tuff for you to strive in this industry. Example: Many sellers are not able to adapt social media henceforth they struggle to connect with younger generations who are available on social media & want to cross check about your services through these platforms.

Sellers who are quick learners, ready to unlearn faster & then relearn with a lot of enthusiasm are the real stars of this industry. They get business from all age segments, professions etc.

Attend all the training programs provided by your company but don't be dependant only on your company training programs. Invest your time & money to learn from outside as well through various online & offline platforms. They are many platforms to hone your skills continuously.

You can read books, watch YouTube channels etc. to learn more.

Write 3 things which you would like to learn in the next 3 months:

1. ....

2. ....

3. ....

CHAPTER FOURTEEN

Identify the Right Target Segment

Don't start approaching people randomly. You need to decide the right target segment who can be your future probable customers with least possible efforts & money.

Here are a few parameters which can help you to choose the right target segment:

• **Area** – Think long term, what is the demographic area which can be served by you easily & efficiently e.g. If you are based out of a metro city, you may decide to serve within that metro city itself or a limited area of that metro city. If you are based out of a small city / town, you may decide to pick up area within 50 kilometres radius.

• **Profession** – You may decide to serve business people or salaried people or both. Go to the next level e.g., if you decide to serve business people, pick up industries which you can relate to (where you worked in the past or you understand these industries well), if you decide to serve salaried people, who they are like private job, government job etc.

• **Role** – Ask yourself, do I relate with all business people / salaried people or with specific roles only e.g., if you are targeting business people, what will be their role like small shopkeepers, factory owners, big business owners etc. Same way, if you are targeting salaried people, what is their role like they are in the beginning of their career like executives, middle management or top management people etc.

• **Family income** – Family income means income from all sources including spouse, parents, kids, sibling if they are living with your prospects. You can divide your prospects into various income groups like family income of less than Rs 5 lakh, Rs 5 lakh to 9.99 lakh, Rs 10 lakh to 19.99 lakh, Rs 20 lakh to 49.99 lakh, Rs 50 lakh to 99.99 lakh, Rs 1 Cr & above... Pick up top 3 income groups where you got maximum success or can relate to.

• **Age bracket** – Divide your prospects into the age bracket of 18-30, 31-40, 41-50, 51-60, 61 & above etc. Check where you feel more comfortable, confident & can relate to? Pick up those 2-3 age brackets to start with e.g. If I am 35, my top priority should be the age bracket of 31-40, then 41-50 & 18-30. Normally, you are most successful within the age group of 10 years younger & older than you. If you are 35, your maximum success comes from the age group of 25 to 45 so you should focus on this age group people.

• **Family life cycle** – There are various family life cycles e.g., single, married with no kids, married with one kid, married with two kids, married with grown up kids, single parent, divorced, retired etc. Pick up 2-3 segments where you can relate maximum & work on those segments.

• **Gender** – Pick up gender where you got maximum success in the past in any of the roles. There are many people who are not comfortable in getting success in the same gender or opposite gender. There are a few people who are equally comfortable with all genders. Introspect your past performance & comfort level.

• **Religion** – You can also pick up your prospects depending upon on the religion. A few people are comfortable in dealing with people from all religions while there are a few sellers who are not comfortable in dealing with religions other than the religion they follow.

Pick up top 2 target segments if it's not done yet:

Criteria for target segment 1:

Area:
Profession:
Role:
Family Income:
Age bracket:
Family Life Cycle:
Gender:
Religion:

Criteria for target segment 2:

Area:
Profession:
Role:
Family Income:
Age bracket:
Family Life Cycle:
Gender:
Religion:

CHAPTER FIFTEEN

Networking

Remember, **your network is your net worth.**
I have seen that life insurance sellers who do have better network, are more successful than those who have poor network.

You can also work on your networking skills by doing any of the following:

• **Connection request** – You can approach your target segment prospects through social media & can send them connection requests. Don't immediately ask for the business or appointment after you get connected with them. Give them some time to know about you, your services & your achievements.

• **Work on your visibility** – Attend social events like marriages, anniversaries, birthday parties, death rituals, blood donation camps etc in the area as selected by you during the target segment selection.

• **Create a personal brand for yourself** – You can use social media to create your personal brand by making people aware about life insurance, your services, your achievements, feedback from the existing customers etc.

• **Join clubs & networking events** – Find out common clubs between your target market & yourself. Attend such clubs by paying the professional fees like BNI (Business Networking International), Rotary, Lions clubs etc. Join networking events like attending various training programs where you meet other like-minded people.

• Attend PTM (Parent Teacher Meetings), Society meetings: Attend PTMs, society meetings etc. Speak to other parents & society members during such meetings. Make people aware about your profession & services.

• There are thousand of ways to do networking. Keep working on the same consciously.

What are the 3 networking ways on which you will start working immediately:

1. ....

2. ....

3. ....

CHAPTER SIXTEEN

Find out Your Niche

There are so many options within the life insurance, you need to find out your niche. It's like Pareto principle i.e., top 20% products which contribute 80% of your sales. Put your entire energy & efforts in refining & pitching these solutions. You can become a subject matter expert in this category.

You can pick up any 2-3 options for which you have a mastery:

• Child Education solutions
• Child Marriage solutions
• Wealth Creation solutions
• Protection solutions
• Retirement (Pension & Annuity) solutions
• MWPA – Married Women Property Act solutions
• HUF – Hindu Undivided Family solutions
• Key Men Insurance
• Partnership Insurance
• Employer Employee Insurance
• Business Insurance

What are your niche areas on which you will start working immediately:

1. ....
2. ....
3. ....

CHAPTER SEVENTEEN

Know Your Customer

It's always better to know your customer before you approach them. It will help you to connect them in a better way.

You can work on the following to know your customers:

• Work profile:
o What your customers do?
o What is the role & responsibilities of your customers?
o What is a typical day looks like for them?
o What are their challenges, struggles, pain areas e.g., attrition can be a painful area for many of your prospects?
o How does the industry work (in which your customer works)?
o When are they free when you can approach & meet them for your proposal?
o What are their approximate earnings?

• Other details as captured in the right target segment like area, gender, family life cycle, age bracket etc. – We already covered it in this book

• You can find these details through the following ways:

o Social media – through LinkedIn, Instagram, Whatsapp Business, You Tube channel, Facebook etc.
o Colleagues / References: Seek information from other known colleagues or the people who referred these names to you

o Company website: Find out company website if available & understand about their industry & roles etc.

o Google / search engines: Type their names or their business names in Google & find out more information

When you know more about your customers; you understand their problems better, it will assist you to connect better with them & provide a better solution.

CHAPTER EIGHTEEN

Diversification

Don't be dependant only on one product. What if, company withdraw it tomorrow. Diversify your risk into different products.

Use the power of product mix. Treat yourself as a flower seller who sells different types of flowers like – Rose, Marigold, Tulips, Lily, Daisy, Lavender etc.

You can also go one level up of diversification. You can also think about selling health & general insurance products.

You can also clear AMFI exam & sell mutual funds too.

It will help you to cross sell & up-sell very effectively.

- **Cross Sell** means if you are selling a life insurance term product, you can also sell other life insurance products / health insurance products / general insurance product to the same customer.

- **Up-sell** means if you are selling a particular life insurance policy e.g. a term policy of Rs 1 Crore then you can 2nd policy of bigger sum assured to the same customer when his / her income increases & s/he need to cover that extra risk.

CHAPTER NINETEEN

Use the Power of Recommendations

Whensoever you visit a new doctor for any of your family members, do you directly visit or ask for recommendations from your colleagues / neighbours / friends / acquaintances etc?

Chances are quite high that you seek recommendations from the people you know. Same is applicable for your future customers. They are also looking for recommendations for you.

You can ask your customers to share their recommendations through a written letter, mail, linkedin recommendation, a short video, google rating, rating on your website etc.

You can share such recommendations to your future customers. It creates a good impression before you meet them in person. You can also share the same during your face-to-face meeting.

I have 40 plus recommendations received through LinkedIn. It helps me to acquire new clients.

Sell Yourself Well

Before you sell your product / services, you sell yourself first.

Work on your grooming, your communication & other skills, your punctuality etc.

Customer buys you first, then your company / brand & in last your product / service.

Keep your tool kit ready as you never know when you will meet a client.

How do you do handshake, how do you handover your visiting card to the prospect etc. create an impression about you.

It matters; how visible you are in the society. More visibility means more familiar is your face & people want to deal with familiar faces.

Ask yourself – How do people remember me when I am not in the room? Work on these areas & you will be a great seller not only for life insurance but for any of the product / services.

CHAPTER TWENTY-ONE

Use Social Media

Use social media to reach maximum of your prospects. People want to deal with familiar faces, subject matter experts so social media plays a pivotal role to make you familiar.

You can make people aware about the following through any of the social media platforms:

o Videos / shorts / articles on the importance of life insurance & its benefits
o Your achievements with reference to life insurance like qualifying for MDRT, other international training conventions
o Feedback messages / videos from the existing clients – it can be the right advice or assistance during various services like maturity / death claims
o Various updates on financial planning & financial instruments
o New certifications / qualifications added by you which will help you to showcase your expertise
o Update about new services / offers

What all you will do to take out maximum out of social media & by when?

1. ....
2. ....
3. ....

CHAPTER TWENTY-TWO

Elevator Pitch

What is an elevator pitch?
• It's a short speech that introduces an individual, business, product or services.
• Concise and exact use of words is particularly important, where a pitch must be
able to sell itself quickly.
• Duration of the elevator pitch – 1 to 3 minutes.

Examples:

Elevator Pitch for sellers who are already MDRT:
• I feel privilege that I am a MDRT advisor, only 1% of life insurance advisors are MDRT advisors across world. MDRT advisors is top most recognition to us that we provide excellent services to our customers.
Elevator Pitch to approach HNI (High Net Worth) people:
• I am a life insurance professional from last 10 years.
• I exclusively cater HNI people like you to diversify their assets and minimize risk.
Elevator Pitch to approach Business people:
• I am an expert in business insurance and help businesses like yours to plan well for future uncertainties.
Elevator Pitch to approach NRIs (Non-Resident Indians):
• I help NRIs like you to get better returns with added advantage of protection.

Elevator Pitch to approach people who looks right fit for retirement:

• I am a pension expert and help people like you to plan for a graceful retirement.

In the last part of your elevator pitch, you can add the following lines:

- To explore; how our services can be beneficial to you and your family, I want to connect with you for a few minutes.

- Shall we meet today evening or tomorrow morning will be more convenient to you?

Create your own elevator pitch for your niche areas:

1. ....

2. ....

3. ....

CHAPTER TWENTY-THREE

The Art of Probing

Use the art of Probing. Use the 5 W & 1 H technique.
5 Ws are:

- What
- Why
- Who
- Where
- When

1 H is:

- How

Examples:

- What are your top most long term financial goals?
- Why it's your top most goal?
- When do you require this money?
- Who all are in your immediate family?
- Where do you see your business in next 5 years?
- How does this solution sounds to you?

Don't work on number of questions but the quality of these questions & how do you ask it.

The right questions will lead to the required answers which will help you to identify the right needs & preparing the right solution.

The right questions connects you better with the prospects. Practice these probing questions with your colleague & connect it with the previous question or answer given by the prospect.

CHAPTER TWENTY-FOUR

Listening Matters

Only asking questions are not enough, listening is equally important like probing.

God has given us 2 ears & 1 mouth which means listen 2/3 time & speak 1/3 time.

Follow the same principle when you are in front of a prospect i.e., you need to speak only 1/3 & customer need to speak for rest 2/3 of the time.

How to increase your listening power:

- Listen with full body - use your body language too like nodding, showing interest, eye contact etc.
- Make notes - Make notes of important points
- Paraphrase important points
- Appreciate good points
- Recap the discussion points
- Seek clarifications when required
- Listen with curiosity
- Ask relevant questions from the topic spoken by the prospect

When you become an active listener, your relationship reach to a different level & relationship plays a pivotal role in every business.

CHAPTER TWENTY-FIVE

Emotional Disturbance

Life insurance is not sold on logic but maily on emotions. I found it absolutely true. If life insurance was sold on the logic then every body could have come to your office, stand in queue & could have bought different policies for different needs. Everybody knows that they will die on one day & that one day can come any day henceforth they require life insurance to protect various financial goals but people don't think in this way.

Most of the people think that others may pass away due to untimely death but it will not happen to them henceforth you need to use the power of emotional disturbance.

For this you require power phrases, stories, activities, sales ideas etc.

My another book "Sell Life Insurance Proudly" is a culmination of 51 stories, ideas, activities, power phrases etc. This book is available through Amazon, Flipkart & Notion Press. Buy it if you have not bought it so far. Use it diligently & increase your sale.

CHAPTER TWENTY-SIX

Win The Trust

You need to win the trust of your prospects so that they become life time clients & brand ambassadors of yours.

Here are a few ways to win the trust of your prospects:

- Speak truth, don't lie.
- Honour your commitments.
- Be proactive rather than reactive.
- Be approachable.
- Provide best solutions which are beneficials for your prospects.
- Think long term & not short term
- Don't share their information with anyone.
- Don't speak bad about them in their absence.

Remember, you are dealing with human beings. People want to do business with trustworty sales people & not with ordinary sales people. Be a trustworthy sales person.

CHAPTER TWENTY-SEVEN

Adapt Technology

This era is of technology. Use it in your favour.

Most of the companies provide you app for policy submissions, tracking, servicing etc. Understand & use it faster.

There are many ways to use the technology like:

- There are many apps which reminds you about various things like birthdays of your prospects, meeting scheduler & reminders
- There are various ways to use the virtual platform like Microsoft teams, zoom, google meet etc.
- You can use ChatGpt to design customised letters, messages, presentation for your prospects
- You can create your own website to create your personal branding
- You can use various platforms like Instagram, YouTube, Facebook to reach unknown prospects & do awareness campaigns

Train More to Learn More

While you are eager to learn, learning takes time.

There is another way to learn faster.

Train other advisors like you on various topics (products, processes, selling skills etc.).

It will help you to learn faster. Your confidence level will be way high than others.

You can train other people through online mode as well.

Same way, you can educate people about the benefits of life insurance through YouTube channel, Insta videos etc.

More you train, more you learn.

What is the first step, will you take to execute the above point & by when?

1. ....

Time Management

Most of the sellers struggle with the time management. They don't know how to priortize & use time effectively.

Here is the way out:

- **Use Pareto principle** - Do those 20% activities first which will give you 80% of the results.
- **Do urgent & important now** e.g., if there is query from underwriter during the last day of the month / contest, you need to resolve it immediately.
- **Scheduling** the not urgent but important tasks - You need to schedule the important but not urgent tasks e.g., all meetings with prospects, follow up calls etc.
- **Delegating** urgent but not important tasks - to your leader, other colleagues e.g., reverting mails. We have shared more details on this topic in the next chapter.
- **Delete** the not urgent & not important tasks e.g. like frequent tea breaks, social media time pass reels etc.

CHAPTER THIRTY

Use the Power of Delegation

You have limited time & so many things to do. You may start complaining about lack of time for everything.

Here comes the power of delegation. Use it in your favour:

o Think what all can be delegated e.g. if you buy vegetables & groceries regularly from the market, can you delegate the same to your family members or use online platforms

o Can you hire one office assistant & delegate some of the services part to him / her & you can focus on getting the fresh business especially during the peak months?

o Can you delegate a few of the things to your office colleagues / leaders for doing the necessary follow up on issuance of your policies & pendency resolution?

o Can you hire a business development person who can approach people to market your services & can create more leads / meetings for you?

You will find that you can delegate many things henceforth you will get more time to focus on the new business & achieve your SMART goals.

What are the 2 tasks which you will delegate, to whom & by when?

1. ....

2. ....

CHAPTER THIRTY-ONE

Seva Bhav (Selfless Service)

While you can increase your MRP (Money, Rewards & Promotions) through life insurance however that's not the only objective to sell life insurance.

Add "Seva Bhav or selfless service" in it when you approach your prospects for life insurance. Life insurance is a great opportunity to serve others.

The moment you add "Seva Bhav" in it, your perspective changes. You don't get angry on people when they say no to life insurance.

Your role is only to make people aware about the importance of life insurance, selling is by-product of it.

See the impact when you approach people with "Seva Bhav."

Celebrate every Milestone

Life is to celebrate small milestones which leads to big milestones. Don't wait only for the big moments to celebrate.

You can celebrate the following milestones:

o When you achieve your monthly / quarterly milestones
o When you achieve any top 3 positions in the branch likc top premium / cases / type of policies contributor
o When you qualify any branch / regional level contest
o When you entcr into a new target segment with first closure
o When you buy anything worth with the life insurance earning e.g., buying a new home / office / car etc.
The more you celebrate; more you get addicted to such successes. You tend to put more efforts to achieve bigger successes in the life.

Decide 3 criteria for yourself to celebrate within the next 3 months?
1. ....
2. ....
3. ....

CHAPTER THIRTY-THREE

Never Say Die Spirit

No day, week, month, quarter or year will be same. There will be ups & downs in between.

You need to follow "Never Say Die Spirit" to deal with it.

Your prospect will say no to you, your proposals etc. They will question mark on your profession & role. They may demean your work & contribution.

Let them do it but you will never give up on this profession.

Remember the power of life insurance & your role.

You will keep working on inputs & outputs will fall in place.

Let me tell you that it's not an easy profession & role. Your work is hard that's why you get more money, rewards & promotions.

When in doubt, read the stories of advisors who did MDRT / COT / TOT for 30 / 35 /40 years consistenly. If they can do it, you can also do it.

Modern Era Life Insurance Sales Process – Selling like a pro

Every business works on the proven processes. Here is the very powerful life insurance sales process relevant to 21st century post covid era which provides high results to the insurance professionals who use it diligently.

It may happen that your prospect has done some parts of the sales process himself / herself & request you to pitch a solution directly. In that case, while you can still attempt for a detailed analysis however if the prospect is not ready for the same then appreciate his / her need & work done so far on the same. In this case, you can come directly to the step requested by the prospect e.g., presenting the solution. Do a basic need analysis to prepare & present the solution. Once closing is done then you can request for a detailed need analysis & future meeting.

There are 7 steps in the sales process:

1. Prospecting
2. Approaching
3. Meet the prospect & need analysis
4. Preparing & presenting the solution
5. Closing
6. Reference taking
7. Customer Service

Within these 7 steps, objection handling can happen anytime so we will cover this at the end of sales process as chapter 8. Same way, reference taking can also happen anytime during the sales process.

Let's explore these steps in details in coming chapters.

CHAPTER THIRTY-FOUR

Prospecting

When we collect names of the probable customers, this process in known as prospecting. Follow the abbreviation **CHAIN** i.e.

Character – There is no moral hazard with the prospect. Prospect is not a proven fraud person.
Health – The insured health is such that life insurance can be taken
Authority – Person is having authority to take a decision
Income – Prospect is having income to buy insurance
Need – Prospect is having a possible need for your solutions

Most of the sellers leave life insurance industry because they don't have enough prospects. You need to keep adding prospect names in your prospect list. There are many traditional & modern ways to keep adding prospects.

Traditional ways:

- **Market skimming** – Noting contact & business details while visiting a market place
- **Newspaper / magazine / cable tv advertisements** – Noting contact & other details for those prospects who advertised in the newspapers / magazines / cable tv etc.
- **Canopy** – Putting canopies in the market places / corporates / other public places & collecting data of interested people
- **Health / blood donation camp** – Conducting health / blood

donation camps at various societies / market places / community halls etc & generating latest leads

- **Drawing competition** – Organising drawing competitions at schools / societies / at your office & rewarding children by inviting their parents.

- **Cookery competition** – Organising cookery shows / competition at societies / common public places & getting the latest leads

- **Stall booking in trade fairs** – You need to book a stall & arrange marketing material to decorate & distribute.

- **Pumplet distribution / paper inserts** – Take permission from your company, put your name, contact number & mail id & contact newspaper vendors to put it in the newspaper for the targeted area. Do it continuously for 3 days.

- **Corporate presentations / awareness campaigns** – Speak to HR departments & take permission to conduct awareness campaigns through canopy / stall in offices or take permission for 30-60 minutes presentation on awareness on life insurance.

- **Market survey** – Market surveys are available on child education, child marriage, wealth creation, protection, retirement planning & other needs. Speak to your company to arrange the same. Alternatively, you can search the survey formats through Google & can create your own surveys through google forms / monkey surveys or hard copies. Conduct these surveys with your prospects to create interest.

- **Cold calling** – Cold calling is to approach those prospects who are totally unknown to you. You may receive their details through google, buying data from various website etc. Success ratio is very less in cold calling. This should be the last option for you. You can do email or sms campaign to approach these people. You need to remove those contact details who falls under "do not call" category. You should be extra cautious while going for cold calling, you need to follow government rules related to it.

   Modern Ways:

- **Registering your services on Just Dial app or website** – You can register your services on justdial / website or similar platforms get leads.

- **Creating customised Google forms** – you can see YouTube videos on "how to create google forms?" Create it & share the link with your prospects. It will work as pre-approach.
- **Social media** like Instagram, LinkedIn, Facebook, YouTube, WhatsApp Business (we already shared ways to increase your presence through social media in this book)
- **Job portals** – Buying data from job portals & then approaching them for life insurance.

I strongly suggest to maintain a database in soft / hard copy as comfortable to you & keep adding new data in it.

Value of a prospect: Whether a prospect gives business or not but every prospect is having a value for you. **Example:** You approach 10 prospects & only 1 agrees to buy a life insurance policy from you with a ticket size of Rs 1,00,000 premium with a 25% commission rate, which means your earning will be Rs 25,000. Divide this earning of Rs 25,000 by 10 prospects so your average earning per prospect is Rs 2,500. If your average ticket size & closing ratio is higher than this value will also be higher.

Consider this point while you approach any of your prospect. Say thank you to them even when they say no to you.

CHAPTER THIRTY-FIVE

Approaching

Approaching is the 2nd step of sales process. Once you have the names of the prospect, you tend to approach them for the next step.

Very successful life insurance sellers suggest to use pre-approach techniques as well, which means that you should not directly approach the prospect but go for the pre-approach & then approach.

Example: You have contact number or mail id of your prospect. You received it from one of your existing customers. You can drop a normal message / WhatsApp message or mail to your prospects about the reference mentioning that you will call him / her within a day or two. Now a days, people don't prefer to pick up phone from the unknown number. This creates familiarity & people prefer to deal with the familiar people.

Sample WhatsApp message as pre-approach:

Dear Rahul,

I got your number from your office colleague Bala who is one of my clients.

He strongly recommended to connect with you & share about the services offered by me.

Keeping this in mind, I will call you tomorrow for 2-3 minutes. You can save my number.

Regards,

Aarav

You can refine it further as per your experience with your prospects.

Tips to approach your prospects:

There are 3 elements of communication:
Verbal – Means words you speak – its weightage is 7%
Vocal – Means how you speak – it's weightage is 38%
Visual – Means body language, gesture, posture etc. – It's weightage is 55%
You may approach your prospects face to face, video call, audio call, audio message or through chat.Remember the following:
• Visual part is having maximum weightage so attempt to approach your prospect in such a way that you can use this element along with vocal & verbal.
• You need to groom well, use positive body language even when it's not visible & smile appropriately.
• It's not important what you say but it's more important how you say so work on your vocal part. Observe how good speakers use vocal part so effectively.
• Create a customised script for every target market handy especially during the initial few calls.
• Sit straight with your note pad, pen or digital tool to note key points during your calling.
• Listen attentively when your prospects speak.
• Handle objections calmly.
• Objective of the call is to take appointment & not to sell during approach call. Appointment can be taken for face-to-face meeting (preferably) or through video call depending upon the comfort level of your prospect & you.
    Sample telephone call script for a prospect who is referred by his colleague:
    Start of the call:
• Good morning / afternoon / evening Sir / Mam – Start with

greetings in the language in which your prospect can connect with you comfortably.

• May I speak with Rahul? – Confirm the name of the person to whom you want to speak. Sometime, other people pick up the call or it goes to wrong number so it's better to confirm the name in the beginning itself. If somebody else pick up the phone, request that person to handover the call to Rahul or seek for the alternate time to connect. Once confirmed that you are speaking with the right person, say...

• Mr. Rahul; I am Aarav, I got your number from your office colleague Bala who strongly recommended to connect with you. Share your name & use reference details appropriately.

• Is this the right time to speak to you? Or can we speak for 2 minutes? – Take permission to speak as your prospects may be engaged somewhere.

Middle of the call or the main part of the call:

• Introduce yourself, your company & your services like I am working with ABC life insurance company as a financial consultant.

Option1: I have provided financial security in the field of child education, child marriage, protection, wealth protection, retirement planning etc. to 100 plus families in the last 2 years & they got immense benefits out of it. I would like to explore how these services can be beneficial for you without any obligation to buy from me.

Option 2: I assist families to achieve their financial goals in the field of child education, child marriage, protection, wealth protection, retirement planning etc. Many families found my services highly useful for their financial goals. I am sure that same will be beneficial for you as well.

Option 3: Customise it as per your expertise like my expertise it in the field of retirement planning & I helped more than 100 people to plan for a dream retirement. I want to meet you to explore whether you planned enough for your dream retirement or if there is any gap in it.

Last part of the call:

Say - Keeping above in mind, I would like to meet you / set a video call for around 30 minutes. Can we do it today evening at 6 PM or tomorrow 11 AM is more convenient to you? Give 2 options after checking your schedule from the earliest possible dates. Make a note of the date & timing given by the prospect. If prospect offers any other date or timing, check your schedule & fix it. Say thank you to your prospect for giving her time for this call.

We will handle objection parts in the objection handling topic.

During the initial few days, you can refer to the scripts written by you. Once you are confident then it will come naturally. Focus on listening & connect with your prospect.

CHAPTER THIRTY-SIX

Meet the Prospect & Need analysis

Part A: Meet the Prospect:

Once you approached the prospect, it is time to meet him / her for a detailed meeting for around 30 minutes. You may have fixed a face to face meet or virtual meet. Here are a few important points which will enable you to take discussion on a positive note.

Important points for Virtual Meeting:

• Confirm the mode of virtual meeting platform during approaching stage e.g., if it's through google meet, zoom, MS teams etc. Pick up one such platform where both prospect & you are comfortable.
• Once platform, date & timing is fixed, you shall book it & share the link to your prospect through mail, message or WhatsApp etc. Don't delegate this task to the prospect.
• Ideally, you shall join the meeting from your laptop & start the meeting 5 minutes before the fixed meeting time. It will allow you to update the software or resolve any technical glitches. You should not join from your mobile & mobile should be your back up in case laptop breaks down in between.
• You should sit either in a meeting room or a silent area where there is no / less noise & no background movements happening visible through camera. It may disturb prospect / your focus.
• Groom well, don't wear casual clothes. You can keep a nice

background where your trophies, certificates are clearly visible. It creates a good positive impression.

• Once the prospect joins, welcome him / her with smile & greetings like namaskar, welcome, good morning / afternoon / evening etc. You can also do digital hi-five. I use it very frequently & it works.

• You can appreciate the prospect on his / her punctuality if s/he joins on time.

• Self-introduction, need analysis questions will be same as given in the next paragraphs of face-to-face meetings.

Important points for face-to-face Meeting:

• Keep your kit ready like laptop / tab / mobile, diary / planner / notebook, pen, visiting card, testimonials from the existing client, sales tool like conversation starters, identity proof that you are associated with the company & your own id proof etc.

• It is always a good idea to remind the prospect about your meeting before you start your journey from your home / office through the appropriate way like calling / WhatsApp message / normal message / mail etc.

• Groom well, work on your grooming etiquettes.

• Plan your journey in such a way that you reach the meeting venue at least 10-15 minutes before the meeting start time. It will help you to observe many points & will provide some clues to do rapport building / need analysis. It will also help you get familiar with the meeting place.

• When you enter to the prospect office / home / any other meeting point, walk confidently & with a smile.

• Sit attentively when offered to sit. Do the handshake if the prospect offers the same or if you feel appropriate else you can start with greetings like namaskar, good morning / afternoon / evening etc.

• Speak in the language in which both prospect & you are comfortable.

• Thank the prospect for sparing his / her time for this meet.

• Ask for water / tea / coffee if the prospect is in your office or a meeting point finalized by you. If prospect asks about the same then you can share your preferred choice of beverages etc.

• If it's a referred call then you can start talking about the person who referred to this prospect. You can share how do you know the referred person etc. If someone else is going with you like your manager then introduce that person as well.

• Read / watch videos on personality types like DISC (Dominance, Influence, Steadiness & Conscientiousness). Check your own personality type as well through any of the assessments available on the same topic. It will enable you to understand the personality type of your prospect, understand their requirement & connect accordingly.

• You can do rapport building on various topics about the prospect's business / job / family members or his / her won personality, educational background, hobbies, common area of interest etc.

• Rapport building is not a necessary step but an additional tool to connect better with the prospect.

• At this time, you can handover your visiting card to your prospect. You can keep your visiting card in a visiting card holder or in your diary / upper pocket. Give your visiting card with a lot of respect preferably by holding it in both of your hands. At this time, you can also seek the visiting card of the prospect.

   • **You can start by your own introduction where you can include the following:**

o Your full name

o Your role in the life insurance company (like advisor / front line sales person)

o Your vintage in the company

o Your education background & certifications relevant to the life insurance industry

o Your key achievements with the company

o Your mission statement or the reason behind joining this industry o Your family & city / place of living

Example of self intro: I am Harry, serving as insurance advisor / financial consultant with ABC life insurance company. My role is to empower people to achieve their financial goals. I am associated with this company from last 5 years. My overall work experience is 25 years.

I am an MBA & completed my Associateship from Insurance Institute of India. I qualified for MDRT club for the last 3 years & empowered more than 100 families to achieve their financial goals. I joined this industry to make people aware about the benefits of proper financial planning with the help of life insurance. I am living in Faridabad city, sector 21-C from last 17 years. On personal front, I am married, my wife is a tutor. We are blessed with 2 daughters aged 18 & 13.

Note: You should share the information which creates a positive impact about you. Don't lie. You can keep silent on a few points if it's not creating a good impression about you e.g., if you joined your current life insurance company just one month back then no need to mention it. You can highlight your overall work experience or education background.

Once your introduction is done, you can request your prospect to share his / her details. You can pick up a few points from his / her visiting card. At this time, you can ask for his / her profession, family background etc.

Part B: Need Analysis (For Personal Financial Goals):

You can say the following – My role is like a doctor; to provide customised solutions to you, I need to collect some information from you which will be confidential between you, me & our company. I also want to make the note of the same. With your permission, shall we go ahead?

Once the prospect shares his / her consent then you need to use your probing skills in the consultative way. You can read / see videos on SPIN (Situation Questions, Problem Questions, Implication Questions & Need Pay-off Questions) selling or many other selling techniques & use the same for doing the need analysis.

You can start like this & keep writing answers in front of the question asked. I am sharing a few sample probing questions for your ready reference:

• As per the official documents, what's your full name & date of birth?
• What's your current occupation, your role & your workplace address?
• Who all are there in your immediate family?
• What's their name, date of birth, relationship with you & occupation?
• What are your monthly household expenses including education expenses, utility bills, EMIs (Equated Monthly Instalment) except savings?
• What is your current life insurance cover with insurer name, purpose of taking these policies, annual premium amount, policy term, premium paying term, type of policy, current policy status like lapsed or in-force, rider details if opted etc.
• Have you taken any loans? If yes, what was the purpose of taking this loan, what is the outstanding loan amount, EMI amount, pending tenure, insured or not etc.
• What are your current savings / investments, purpose of these savings, expected returns, saving frequency, expected maturity date etc.

Say – My specialisation is in the field of providing need-based / customised solutions for child education, child marriage, wealth creation, retirement planning, protecting standard of living etc. Out of these goals, what is the top most goal where you see maximum gap. As prospect responds, you can pick up that area & ask relevant questions to explore further. Keep making notes.

If your prospect says, child education goal then start with this goal else do it as per the top goal mentioned by the prospect. Once first goal discussion happens then you can move to the 2nd priority goal. Ideally, you should not discuss more than 2 goals in one meeting.

Child education goal:

As mentioned earlier, you shared that you have 2 kids A & B. On which child, we shall discuss first. If the prospect says child A then start asking questions as following:

A is currently 10 years old (use child's name as mentioned earlier along with the age), at what age do you see that you would be requiring money for his / her higher education goals?

Whether you would be requiring this money in one go or in a span of 3-4 years?

What is the present / current value of this goal?

What should I take inflation rate for this goal as inflation rate is comparatively higher for higher education expenses?

Out of the life insurance policies taken, have you dedicated any specific policy for this goal? If yes, which one? Tell me more about this policy like policy term, maturity date, expected maturity value etc.

Out of the savings / lumpsum investment mentioned earlier, what are the savings / investment done exclusively for this goal?

What is the current value of these savings / investments, saving frequency & amount, type of instrument, expected return etc.?

What is the expected maturity amount when you will be requiring this money for your child's higher education goal?

What is your risk appetite to achieve the gap area? Would you like to go for a fully guaranteed instrument for this goal, or ready to take moderate risk or will you prefer high-risk instrument?

Once you complete your questions for child A then go for child B in the similar fashion if your prospect says that this is his / her priority number 2. If your prospect is satisfied with the current financial planning for his / her child B then you can skip questions on this need.

Child marriage goal:

You will ask questions as similar to child education. You will replace child education with marriage.

Wealth Creation Goal:

Wealth creation includes a lot of goals e.g., buying a dream home / villa / office / factory / holiday home / a new car / foreign trip / business set up for self / spouse / kids, creating a corpus for donation / charity, emergency fund etc. What are your wealth creation goals?

Once you clarify the wealth creation goal, rest of the questions will be like as asked for child education goals e.g., present value of the goal, inflation rate, existing life insurance policy taken for this goal, current savings, risk appetite etc.

Retirement planning Goal:

Given a choice, at what age would you like to retire from your job / business?

Whether anybody else will be part of this retirement planning e.g., your spouse?

If you retire today, how much money would be required on monthly basis to maintain same standard of life?

What should I take inflation rate for this goal?

Out of the life insurance / pension / annuity policies taken, have you dedicated any specific policy for this goal? If yes, which one? Tell me more about this policy like policy term, maturity date, expected maturity value / pension etc.

Out of the savings / lumpsum investment mentioned earlier, what are the savings / investment done exclusively for this goal e.g., PF (Provident Fund), PPF (Public Provident Fund), Superannuation fund, EPS (Employee Pension Scheme), NPS (National Pension Scheme), Gratuity etc.

What is the current value of these savings / investments, saving frequency & amount, type of instrument, expected return etc.? What is the expected maturity amount when you will be requiring this money for your child's higher education goal?

What is your risk appetite to achieve the gap area? Would you like to go for a fully guaranteed instrument for this goal or ready to take moderate risk or will you prefer high-risk instrument?

Protection Goal or Protecting Standard of Living goal:

1. Say – Earlier, you said that your monthly household expenses including education expenses, utility bills, EMIs (Equated Monthly Instalment) except savings are e.g,, Rs 1 lakh / month....Am I correct?

2. Which means, yearly household expenses are (Multiply monthly household expenses with 12) Rs 1 lakh * 12 = Rs 12 lakh per year .....Am I right? If prospect request you to add / alter this number then do the same.

3. If tomorrow you are not there, what is the expected annual rate of interest from the corpus invested by the family in a safe instrument e.g., FD (Fixed Deposit) rate of interest 6% ....

4. What is the value of all outstanding loans (not covered by insurance) e.g., Rs 20 lakh ....

5. What is the pure / term protection cover taken by you exclusively for this purpose?

6. Please also share policy term, premium paying term, type of cover, rider details, premium frequency, annual premium amount etc.

Once you complete need analysis part (preferably for 2 goals during one meeting) then ask these questions with relevant emotions:

• Why have you kept these goals as number 1 & number 2 priority? Or how important are these goals for you on a scale of 1 to 10 where 1 is lowest & 10 is highest?

• Who all are involved in these goals from your family?

• What will be the feeling of yours / your family once you achieve these goals on time, as per the requirement?

• What if; due to some unforeseen circumstances; you are not able to achieve this goal the way you planned it, how would you feel about it?

• What about your family members, how will they feel about it?

• If these goals are so important for you & your family, what is the monthly / yearly saving amount commitment exclusively for these 2 goals to fulfil the gap (name those 2 goals like your child education & your own retirement planning) ....note down the commitment separately for both goals.

• What is your current health status?

• Have you gone through any major surgeries / treatment in the past?

• Are you taking any regular medications for any of the illnesses?

• In past, is any of your policies were declined by any of the life insurance companies? If yes, what was the reason behind it?

• Whether you would like to become life insured for the proposed solution or do you want to make anybody else as life insured e.g. your child / spouse etc. If yes, request prospect to introduce with these people & take down the relevant details e.g., existing insurance cover etc.

• Do you have any other information to share which can be valuable for this purpose?

Part B: Need Analysis (for Business Insurance Goals):

Key Men Policies:

• Are you aware about the key men policy & about its working including taxation rules etc?

• As per you, why key men policy is important for your company?

• What will be the impact of the death of the key men if you don't have key men policy?

• Would you like to mitigate this risk?

• What is your gross & net profit for the last 3 years?
• Have you taken any existing key men insurance for any of your key men? If yes, please share the relevant details like cover amount, policy term, premium paying term, insurer, type of policy etc.
• How many key men are there in your company? Can I know their name, gender, date of birth, their role, annual salary, retirement age, personal insurance cover of key men etc.
• What is the cover amount which you are looking for these key men?
• Have you thought about any specific budget for the above cover required for your key men? If yes, please share the same.

Partnership Insurance:

• Replace key men with partnership insurance. Most of the other points will be same.
Employer Employee Insurance scheme:
• Are you aware about the employer employee policy & about its working including taxation rules?
• As per you, why employer employee policy is important for your company?
• What are the various ways which you have adapted to retain your critical employees?
• What if your critical employees leave you in between & goes to the competitor, how it will impact your future growth / survival of the business?
• Would you like to mitigate this risk?
• Have you taken any existing employer employee policies for any of your employees? If yes, please share the relevant details like cover amount, policy term, premium paying term, insurer, type of policy etc.
• How many employees, you want to cover at present through employer employee policies?
• What is the cover amount, type of policy etc which you are looking for these employees?

• Have you thought about any specific budget for the above cover required for your employee? If yes, please share the same.
• We would be requiring full details of your employees in a format to be shared by me.

If you are doing business insurance call for the first time, I strongly recommend you to take support from any of your seniors / colleagues who are familiar with the business insurance process. Once you observe 2-3 calls then you can start conducting these calls independently.

Do remember that rapport building is an ongoing thing so keep finding out opportunities to do rapport building through out the need analysis stage & natural appreciation too.

Once need analysis is done, you can say:

Share summary of the meeting & take confirmation for your understanding.

Dear Sir / Mam, thank you so much for your valuable time & providing all the relevant details. I need some time to prepare a customised solution for the same. Shall we meet tomorrow evening / day after tomorrow morning where I can present this customised solution to you. Fix the exact date, time, venue etc. If it's a virtual meeting then fix the same & share the link to the prospect. Remind him / her few hours before the next meeting time.

CHAPTER THIRTY-SEVEN

Preparing & Presenting the solution

Part 1: Prepare the solution:

Treat your self as a doctor. You collected all the relevant information or you have done diagnosis. Now you need to suggest the medicines / treatment. You need to decide the dose (type of policy) & frequency as per the need of your patient / prospect.

You need to do the following:

• Check whether all the information is collected properly
• If not or you need any clarifications, call / message prospect & take the clarity / remaining information
• Use any of the financial calculator available through internet / apps & calculate the future value of all goals
• Same way, calculate the future / maturity value of all savings / investment / existing policies done by the prospect
• Reduce these savings / maturity value from the future value of goals & calculate the gap
• Depending upon the gap, pick up the right policy with the right policy term, premium paying term, cover amount, riders, take customised benefit illustrations etc.
• You can prepare 2 sets of the solution:
o Set 1 can be the ideal solution to fill the gap fully
o Set 2 can be as per the committed saving amount or as per the

budget of the prospect which may not fill the gap fully but partially
• You can pick up / save other supporting material like brochures, testimonials by the existing clients, comparisons chart with the key competitor products / instruments etc.
• You can also prepare the possible objections & how to resolve these objections

Part 2: Presenting the solution:

o Repeat all the relevant steps as done during first meeting like reminder for the meeting

o Share summary of the first meeting

o Present solution of the top priority goal first

o Use time line, use names, use FAB (Feature, Advantage, Benefits) technique to pitch your solution e.g.,

o **Feature** – Limited Premium Payment option

o **Advantage** – You need to pay only for first 5 / 7 / 10 years of policy instead of full policy term of 15 / 20 / 25 years.

o **Benefits** – No long-term commitment to pay for 20 / 25 years. Fulfilling the goal by paying only for the initial few years. No tension of continuing of policy due to any uncertainty in future income due to job / business losses

o Keep your focus on explaining those benefits which are more relevant to your prospect.

o Pitch the ideal solution first i.e. set 1 which covers the full gap.

o Keep asking for the prospect feedback & his / her liking about the benefits.

o Once you cover major benefits, ask your prospect about the key benefits liked by him / her. Explain it again if require. Involve family member names for whom these solutions have been pitched. Relate it back to the feeling questions asked during the need analysis stage like – Sir / Mam, you said that you & your family will feel top of the world once you are able to achieve this goal. This customised solution will ensure that you achieve your goal of your son / daughter higher education etc.

o You may have prepared a combo of 2 products for the above

solution. Explain combo benefits first. During the last stage of the solution pitching, you can highlight that these are 2 separate policies which will give you the required benefits as per your need. It can be 2 or 3 separate policies with separate policy terms, premium payment terms, insurance cover etc but your focus is on to provide the customised solution. You can relate it like a doctor who prescribes tablets, capsules, syrups, injections etc as per the diagnosis. Your focus has to be proper treatment which may happen from one policy, 2 policies or more than 2 policies.

o You can also show relevant brochure, past performances of bonuses / returns, testimonials etc. as per the requirement. You can share the authentic material through mail / WhatsApp as well or show it through your company website if it's given on your company website.

o Keep doing rapport building in between. You can also mention about other prospects with similar needs, who decided to go for these solutions.

o Premium should be disclosed in the last part of solution pitching, pitch premium as monthly saving amount & then go for the annual saving amount. Remember, you have taken monthly commitment during the need analysis stage so it will link to that easily.

o If prospect objects or shows helplessness about premium paying capacity then pitch set 2 solutions as per the budget shared by the prospect.

o **Ask your prospect about the feedback for the solutions presented by you.**

CHAPTER THIRTY-EIGHT

Closing

So far, you have done a good job by doing a proper need analysis & pitching a customised solution to your prospect. You already have done many closings like asking time for the first, second meeting, about solutions etc. These small closings are now leading to a big closing.

It may happen that your prospect asks you for the next step or showing his / her eagerness to buy the policies.

If not, you can initiate the closing. That's the natural outcome of your meeting with your prospects. It has to be natural & gilt free. Remember, you are not asking anything for your personal benefits. You are just a medium who is assisting a prospect to achieve his / her financial goals. If you will not do it somebody else will do it & that somebody else may not recommend a good solution as you can. Trust your capabilities & your work.

Various Ways to close the call:

You may visit YouTube, Google, Chatgpt or other social media platforms to find out various ways to close the sales call & keep experimenting with the same. I am sharing a few ways of closing which I found very effective & the same is used by thousands of life insurance sellers. Here are some of the closing techniques, you may use it as at is or with some modifications.

- **Assumptive Close**: Asking question/s by assuming that prospect is ready to buy policies from you
o Examples:
o Who will be the nominee for these policies?
o How would you like to pay for this policy – through UPI / Debit Card / Credit Card / Net Banking / Cheque or any other way?
o Shall I keep premium frequency as half yearly or yearly?
o Can I request you to share your Aadhar card number details to submit the application form
o Shall we keep sum assured as Rs 90 lakh or can we make it as Rs 1 crore?

- **1-2-3 close:**
o Summarize in sets of three items. We will give you this, that and the other.
o This may be features of the service, benefits or add-on sweetener items.
o Most customers want services that are economical, perfect, and available now. This is the classic business measurement trilogy of cost, quality and time.
o Example: This solution is providing high insurance cover, it's within your budget & providing guaranteed maturity amount equal to the goal amount for your child's higher education goal.
o It's like a quick recap cum reinforcement of the solution pitched by you.
o In the last – You can ask, do you have any other questions or shall we proceed for the closing formalities?

- **Compliment close:**
o Be nice to them. Tell them how wonderful they are. Be amazed and impressed by them. Also compliment them on previous decisions, although you can also appreciate their need for a new one.
o Example: Well; as you are so knowledgeable & smart, you will

understand better how good this decision is for you & your loved ones.

o In the last – You can ask, do you have any other questions or shall we proceed for the closing formalities?

• **Best time close:**

o When people are procrastinating or will 'be back', emphasize how now is the best time to buy.

o All life insurance sales people know that 'there are no be backs'.

o Examples:

o There is no 'best time to buy life insurance' which makes now the best time.

o The best time to take admission is now, whilst you are in good health. What if there are any health issues in the coming days. You may not get insurance at all or pay very high premium for the same cover.

o There can be an upward revision in the premiums or downward revision in the bonuses in the coming days.

o This policy is available for a limiter period only & it may be withdrawn by the company anytime.

You can also try to increase cover, premium, pitching 2nd policy by the following ways:

- Dear sir / mam, currently you have chosen a cover of Rs 1.8 Crore, if you make it to Rs 2 Crore then you get a large sum assured discount on the premium. By paying a neglible extra premium, your risk cover will be increase by 20 lakhs? Shall we go ahead?

- Dear sir / mam, currently you have chosen a premium of Rs 85 k per annum, can we make it Rs 1 lakh per annum as it will be easier for you to remember plus you will get higher benefits. Shall we go ahead?

- Thanks for taking this decision of going ahead. I strongly recommend to go ahead with your 2nd priority goal of retirement planning along with this goal. The sooner, the better it will be for you.

o In the last – You can ask, do you have any other questions or shall we proceed for the closing formalities?

Most of the companies have online system in place to submit the application forms on behalf of the prospects. They need to share OTPs to you for their consent else they themselves can submit the application forms.

Add all relevant documents like KYC documents – Aadhar card copy, PAN card copy, latest colour photo, bank account details or cancel cheque copy, income proof etc. after thoroughly checking it.

Assist prospect to pay the premium as per the payment method chosen by him / her.

Tell them clearly that premium will be on hold & their risk will not commence till the underwriter assess the risk & issue the policy.

Tell them about the medical requirement if any & process for the medicals.

Tell them about the total days required to issue the policy & requirement for additional documents if required by the underwriter.

Tell them that how they will get their policy document. Most of the companies send the PDF copy of the policy document & same happens through Insurance Repositories (IR) like NSDL.

Tell them about the **freelook period** in which they can review the policy & terminate it in case they did not like the solution.

You can also share customer helpline number, WhatsApp Helpline number, helpline mail id & nearest branch address etc. in case of urgency.

You may ask for emergency numbers of the prospect to whom you can approach him / her in case his / her number is not approachable. You can also request your prospect to introduce you with his / her nominee or the person who can contact you in case of emergency.

CHAPTER THIRTY-NINE

Reference Taking

Reference taking is like taking the balance money from a shopkeeper to whom you gave Rs 500 note to buy a product worth Rs 100. You need to take Rs 400 back as that's your right.

If you have done a good work with your prospect then s/he may refer your name automatically to his / her circle. Referral business is one of the most powerful ways of approaching new prospects.

You may ask referrals during any stage of the sales process e.g., during the telephone appointment when the prospect says that s/he is not insurable / interested as of now then you can seek for the references.

Same way, you can seek references during the first meeting or second meeting or any follow up meetings.

You can also seek feedback for your services before asking for the references.

Here are a few pitches which can be used for asking references:

o **Straight forward request for references** – Say, my business runs on references. I got your reference from ABC. Same way, I need 3 references from you to whom I can approach. I would like to ensure you that I will provide similar professional services to them & I will not share any of your personal details with them.

o **Using prompters** – You can also use prompters (hints) when your prospect is not able to relate any names. Here are a few **examples**:
o During our call, you mentioned your office colleague name DEF. Do you think that s/he will be the right fit as a prospect for my services?
o Do you recall a few names from your workplace / business?
o You can think about people from your neighbourhood.
o People who are in private / government job & known to you.
o People who are your service providers like vendors, drycleaners etc.
o Professional people like doctors, tax consultants, Chartered accountants etc.\

o More details you get, better it's for you so focus on getting maximum information about the prospects like relationship with the prospect, their profession, family background, place of living, possible needs etc.
o You can also request your prospect to give these references a call-in front of you & talk about your services. Your prospect can also mention that they can expect your call in the coming 1-2 days' time.

o You can use approaching / pre-approach techniques as mentioned earlier to approach these references.
o You shall also share the timely progress on these leads with your prospect who referred these leads.
   Safe exit – Your prospect / customer is not ready to give you any references, you can find out a safe exit by saying, "Dear sir / mam, While I understand that you don't want to share or you don't have time or you don't remember these names as of now, can I request you to share once you are comfortable to share these references. I will approach you after a few days for the same." Be in touch with your prospect & speak to him / her at the appropriate time to get references.

CHAPTER FORTY

Customer Service

No sale is complete if you don't provide excellent customer services.

Use the formula of under commit & over deliver.

Here are a few techniques which can assist you to make it more impactful:

o **Segmentation** – Divide your customers into different segments / buckets depending upon their contribution in your business. Top business contributor can be of top priority, medium contributor as medium priority & bottom contributors as bottom priority.

o **Differential treatment** – Once segmentation is done, you should treat them differently e.g., you can meet your top priority customers in good cafes / restaurants once in a month / quarterly, wish their birthdays / anniversaries with flower bouquet / cakes, special customised wishes etc.

o **Set service benchmarks** – You can set your personal service benchmarks like reverting to each requirement within 24 hours. You can help them to pay renewals on time, time to time update on their policy & services offered by the company.

o **Claim settlement** – This should be the top most priority for you whether it's maturity, survival or death claims. You need to assist them proactively not only for the policies bought from you but from other life insurance companies as well.

o **Giving references** – While many sales people focus only on getting references, you shall focus on giving references to your prospects at personal / professional level. More you give, you will get more.

o **Stay in touch & approachable** – The most important part of your business is that you need to stay in touch with your prospects & be approachable.

o **Connect through social media** – You can also connect with your prospects through social media, find out opportunities to appreciate their work / contribution, wishing them on various occasions.

Your need to provide such customer services so that your customer becomes your brand ambassador. Keep exceeding the expectations of your customers & see how your business multiply.

CHAPTER FORTY-ONE

Objection Handling

Before you read further, there is a question for you – Do you buy all products / services offered by every sales person in your life?

I am yet to meet a person who buys all the products / services offered by every sales person. I put a lot of objections before buying any product / services. Even if a sales person handles all the objections, then also, I don't buy every product / service immediately due to various reasons.

Keep the above perspective clear, whatsoever best you are offering, it may not relevant to every body now or in future. When people are giving objections, they are not rejecting you but the services offered by you due to hundred of reasons best known to them only.

If you follow the first 7 steps of sales process well, you may not get objections at all or may get a very few objections. Your prospects may ask queries but queries are different from the objections.

Let me share a few queries:

o What is the minimum premium amount for this policy?
o Does this policy allow only yearly mode of payment or half-yearly option is also available?
o What are the past bonus rates / last 5 years returns for this product?
o How this product is better than the other competitor products?

These above examples are of queries which need to be answered with your knowledge. It's like asking your date of birth & then you tell a person about your date of birth without thinking much.

Why Objection comes? - Go deeper & think why objection comes?

Objection may come due to any of the following reasons:

o Prospect is not fully convinced about the product / your company / you.
o Prospect wants best possible deal
o Prospect is not ready at present & wants to postpone the decision for future
o It's natural tendency for many prospects to keep postponing hence they put an objection
o It may happen due to confusion as prospect is thinking about various options pitched to him / her
o Prospect wants more time to study the pro & cons of taking this decision as this decision is for a longer duration & any wrong decision can backfire him / her
o Prospect is really concerned for the future of his / her near & dear ones & wants to check all aspects of the solution offered by you

Please understand that objection handling is a skill which can be learnt. If you don't handle these objections, somebody else will handle it, will close the sales call & get business.

How to handle objections –

Objection Handling Technique during approaching stage –

Example -
FFF (Feel Felt Found) – This is very famous techniques & many sales people use it very effectively during telephone appointment e.g.,
Objection: I don't need life insurance

Feel: I understand that you feel that you don't need life insurance
Felt: Many of my existing customers felt in the same way, till they met me
Found: Once we met for 30 minutes, they found my services highly beneficial & now they are doing business with me. I just want to do a proper need analysis. This will be a double check for you for your important financial goals. I will congratulate you if everything is in place. Even if, I find a gap, I will not force you to buy anything from me, going ahead with my services will be purely optional. Keeping this in mind, can we meet ......

You can handle many of the similar objections with FFF technique. Do remember, your end goal during approaching stage is get an appointment & not to sell life insurance. Make your prospect comfortable by telling them that you will not force them at any stage to buy life insurance from you.

Objection handling technique during presenting solution / closing / reference taking:
    ACC – Acknowledge, Counter & Close

Example:
Objection: Your product returns are low than the competitor products:
Acknowledge – I appreciate your concern that you think that our product is offering lower returns than the competitor products
Counter – What are the top most benefits which you liked about our product? You may get better returns with the competitor products however return is not the only criteria to compare one product with another. One should also look into the other aspects of the solution like safety, liquidity, risk cover, guaranteed vs non-guaranteed benefits, claim settlement ratios etc. Overall, this product is providing best in class benefits as per your need.
    Close – Do you have any other questions to ask? If not let's complete the closing formalities.

Mix of Rational & Emotional Approach –

You should use a mix of rational & emotional approach to handle objections. You can use the names of the family members for whom this policy will be beneficial, you can rephrase the feeling part as shared by the prospect earlier.

Straightforward approach –

Many of the sales people handle it straight forward.
Example – Your premium rates are more than the market rates.
Straight forward approach answer – Yes sir / mam, Our premium rates are more than the market rates because we are the premier life insurer. Our services are world class e.g., we settle claims with 24 hours while other settles it in 7 days. We provide door step services, you or your family need not to visit anywhere, we come to your door step for every single service.

You can prepare a list of all possible objections & prepare ways to handle these objections with calmness. There is no one full proof technique, observe other successful sales people, learn from them, attend more training programs & keep experimenting with these techniques.

Prepare a list of all possible objections, contact your branch trainer / sales supervisor or other colleague to get the list & practice it. I am sharing a few comparisons with other asset class:

Objection: Equity or Mutual Funds are better than the Life Insurance:

- Equity / Mutual Funds does not give only high returns but it also comes with **high risk.**
- You may be an **expert** in equity / mutual funds but **what about your family?** Are they equally competent to handle equity / mutual funds portfolio in your absence?

- Equity / mutual funds are good for getting higher returns. I appreciate that you have a good knowledge about it. What if market goes downwards & you require funds for your important goals? You have seen the downfall during covid.
- I am not asking to invest 100% of your investments in the life insurance but only some part of your investment so that you get benefits of diversification. While you should invest some part of your portfolio in it but not the entire investment.
- Life insurance guarantees your goal from day 1. Equity / mutual funds may give you higher returns, what if you are not there tomorrow? Can they guarantee your important goals in your absence? They can fulfil these goals if you are there tomorrow & keep investing in it regularly.

Objection: Bit coins are better than the life insurance:

- Dear Sir / mam, Ask yourself - If bit coins regulated the way life insurance is regulated in India?
- Does it carry high risk along with the righ returns? Is it safe?
- Is your family equally competent like you to handle it diligently?
- What if I require this money after 10 years & bit coin market is totally down?
- Can you put 100% of your investment in a single tool?

Objection: Real Esate is better than the life insurance:

- Dear sir / mam, what are the risks associated with the real estate? Listen to the points shared by your prospect.
- What if you require a small corpus, whether you will sell your whole property to meet that need?
- What if somebody gets hold of your property & there are legal disputes on it?
- Is your family equally competent like you to handle it diligently?
- I am not asking to invest 100% of your investments in the life insurance but only some part of your investment so that you get

benefits of diversification. While you should invest some part of your portfolio in it but not the entire investment.

Objection: Gold is better than the life insurance:

- Dear sir / mam, what are the risks associated with the physical gold or ornamental gold (as told by the prospect)? Listen to the points shared by your prospect.
- I am not asking to invest 100% of your investments in the life insurance but only some part of your investment so that you get benefits of diversification. While you should invest some part of your portfolio in it but not the entire investment.
- Emotional attachment to the gold is very high & one would not like to sell it for future financial goals. Ornaments have lesser values than the 24 carat gold.
- Physical gold also comes with a risk of getting stolen if kept at home.

What worked with one prospect may not work with another prospect.

Abbreviations

MDRT – Million Dollar Round Table
COT – Court of the Table
TOT – Top of the Table
LIC – Life Insurance Corporation
UPI – Unified Payment Interface
ULIP – Unit Linked Insurance Plan
IRDAI – Insurance Regulatory & Development Authority of India
IR – Insurance Repositories
NSDL – National Securities Depository Limited
PDF – Portable Document Format
MBA – Master of Business Administration
B.Com – Bachelor of Commerce
AIII – Associateship from Insurance Institute of India
FIII - Fellowship from Insurance Institute of India
SMART–Specific, Measurable, Achievable, Realistic, Time bound
OAR - Observer, Action, Result
OTP – One Time Password
KYC – Know Your Customer
HR – Human Resources
PAN – Permanent Account Number

Disclaimer

To protect the privacy of certain individuals the names and identifying details have been changed. This is a work of fiction. Any names or characters, businesses or places, events or incidents, are fictitious. Any resemblance to actual persons, living or dead, or actual events is purely coincidental.

It is notified that neither the content provider nor the editor or any person related with this book in any manner shall be responsible for any damage or loss of action to anyone, of any kind, in any manner, therefrom.

How To Contact The Author

First of all, please accept my sincere thanks for investing your time to buy & read this book.

If you like it, do share about this book to others. Gift this book to others.

If you have any feedback, views to share with the author then the author can be approached through the following mail id: failthefailure2@gmail.com

You can contact through the same mail id for any inquiry on content development, training delivery, fire walk activity or motivational speech.

Once again, thank you so much for being part of my life journey.

Lots of blessings and love.

From: Harbans Lal Arora

www.ingramcontent.com/pod-product-compliance
Lightning Source LLC
Chambersburg PA
CBHW031647170726
47990CB00019B/2672